Savvy

Girls Rock

GIRLS ROCK!

Amazing Tales of Women in Music

by Shelley Tougas

Consultant: James Henke
former chief curator for the Rock and Roll Hall of Fame
and author of several books, including biographies of
John Lennon, Bob Marley, and Jim Morrison

CAPSTONE PRESS
a capstone imprint

Savvy Books are published by Capstone Press,
1710 Roe Crest Drive, North Mankato, Minnesota 56003
www.capstonepub.com

Library of Congress Cataloging-in-Publication Data
Tougas, Shelley.
 Girls rock! : amazing tales of women in music / by Shelley Tougas.
  pages cm.—(Savvy. Girls Rock!)
 Includes bibliographical references and index.
 Summary: "Through narrative stories, explores female musicians who have made major contributions to music and culture"—Provided by publisher.
 ISBN 978-1-4765-0234-2 (library binding) ISBN 978-1-4765-3564-7 (eBook PDF)
 1. Women musicians—Juvenile literature. I. Title.
 ML3929.T68 2014
 780.82—dc23   2012046448

Editorial Credits
Jennifer Besel, editor; Veronica Scott, designer; Svetlana Zhurkin, media researcher; Laura Manthe, production specialist

Photo Credits
Corbis, 38 (bottom), 57, Leif Skoogfors, 59 (top), Lynn Goldsmith, 24, Wally McNamee, 23 (bottom); Dreamstime: Stefan Dumitru, 28 (middle); Getty Images: AFP, 23 (right), George Rose, 21 (front), Michael Ochs Archives, 16 (left), Redferns, 45, Time Life Pictures/Barbara Laing, 37, Walter Iooss Jr., 15; iStockphotos: GYI NSEA, 34, 50 (top), 55 (right); Library of Congress, 18, 27; Newscom: ABACA/Slaven Vlasic, 13, AFP/Bob Strong, 49, AFP/Gerard Burkhart, 28 (top), Album, 44, Album/Paramount Pictures, 33 (left), Beitia Archives Digital Press Photos, 7 (top and bottom), Mirrorpix, 6, 46, Mirrorpix/Draper, 47, Mirrorpix/Nigel Wright, 9 (right), Mirrorpix/Ward McNeill, 29 (middle), Splash News/Jennifer Mitchell, 8 (left), WENN Photos/JM11, 33 (right), ZUMA Press/Boris Spremo, 59 (bottom), ZUMA Press/Douglas Kent Hall, 40–41, ZUMA Press/Karen Pulfer Focht, 61 (front), ZUMA Press/Keystone Pictures USA, 30, ZUMA Press/LAMedia, 42, ZUMA Press/Sunshine/Stillphoto, 5 (right), ZUMA Press/Toronto Star/Ken Faught, 16 (right); Shutterstock, cover, back cover, 1, 3 song photography, 52, 578foot, 4, 5 (left), Absent A, 58–59 (back), Aija Lehtonen, 28 (bottom), Allies Interactive, 34–35 (back), 42–43 (back), Anna Paff, 12–13 (back), 64, caricatura, 14, ChinellatoPhoto, 39 (top), cinemafestival, 39 (bottom), Dana Nalbandian, 29 (top), Efecreata Photography, 7 (middle), fat_fa_tin, 3, Featureflash/Paul Smith, 11, Helga Esteb, 60, Iwona Grodzka, 36 (front), jazzia, 25, lem, 16 (back), 17 (back), LittleRambo, 22 (left), 23 (top), Login, 21 (back), Lola Tsvetaeva, 36–37 (back), Maisei Raman, 38 (top), Northfoto, 51 (top), Odelia Cohen, 10–11 (back), optimarc, 59 (middle), Paolo Gianti, 29 (bottom), pashabo, 22-23 (back), Paul McKinnon, 50 (bottom), Pixel Embargo, 62–63, R_lion_O, 30–31 (back), Rachell Coe, 51 (bottom), RAStudio, 8–9, s_bukley, 32, 56, silky, 46–47 (back), stockshoppe, 26–27 (back), 32–33 (back), VolkOFF-ZS-BP, 6 (back), 7 (back), withGod, 61 (back), xzserg, 52–53 (back), YlinPhoto, 54–55; Wikipedia: Hans Hillewaert, 54 (left)

Direct quotations are placed within quotation marks and appear on the following pages. Other pieces written in first-person point of view are works of creative nonfiction by the author.
p3: www.ellafitzgerald.com/about/quotes.html; **p4:** www.npr.org/templates/story/story.php?storyId=16735834; www.brainyquote.com/quotes/authors/j/janis_joplin.html#q2q3u9DiDl8AgTUe.99; **p6:** www.time.com/time/magazine/article/0,9171,957012,00.html; **p8:** www.dailymail.co.uk/tvshowbiz/article-1357439/Janet-Jackson-opens-father-Joe-revealing-interview-Piers-Morgan.html; **p11:** www.imdb.com/name/nm0000659/bio; **p18:** www.legacy.com/ns/news-story.aspx?t=billie-holiday--the-tragic-life-of-lady-day&id=295; **p19:** www.billieholiday.com/about/quotes.htm; **p20:** sports.yahoo.com/blogs/nfl-shutdown-corner/whitney-houston-performed-greatest-national-anthem-sports-history-020851426.html; **p25:** Carlisle, Belinda. Lips Unsealed. (New York: Crown Publishers, 2010); **p28:** www.elle.com/pop-culture/reviews/12-greatest-female-electric-guitarists-339255; thinkexist.com/quotation/my-guitar-is-not-a-thing-it-is-an-extension-of/348409.html; www.npr.org/2011/12/21/144039089/new-tori-amos-cd-night-of-hunters-redefines-classics; toriamos.com/go/galleries/view/516/1/515/press/index.html; www.usatoday.com/life/music/news/story/2012 03 29/bonnie-raitt-interview/54134702/1; www.premierguitar.com/Magazine/Issue/2012/Apr/Bonnie_Raitt_Return_of_te_Blues_Baroness.aspx; **p29:** www.acousticguitar.com/issues/ag81/CoverStory.shtml; www.independent.co.uk/arts-entertainment/music/reviews/norah-jones-lso-st-lukes-london-432192.html; www.brainyquote.com/quotes/authors/n/norah_jones.html; www.guardian.co.uk/music/musicblog/2011/feb/03/white-stripes-fire-fury; **p31:** www.brainyquote.com/quotes/authors/e/ella_fitzgerald.html; www.ellafitzgerald.com/about/quotes.html; **p38:** tmagazine.blogs.nytimes.com/2010/03/08/shes-still-unusual-cyndi-lauper/; **p39:** www.harpersbazaar.com/magazine/cover/the-real-lady-gaga-1011; quoteslyrics.blogspot.com/2009/01/grace-jones-quotes-ii.html; **p41:** Johnson, Robert E. "Gladys Knight and the Pips Still Sizzle After 35 Years Together," Jett Magazine. Jan. 25, 1988; **p50:** www.salon.com/2008/01/30/conversations_crow/; **p51:** www.innerviews.org/inner/difranco.html; **p53:** www.telegraph.co.uk/culture/music/rockandpopfeatures/8062342/Chrissie-Hynde-interview.html; **p54:** articles.orlandosentinel.com/1988-09-06/lifestyle/0060420109_1_tracy-chapman-fast-car-pop-songs; **p55:** www.parade.com/celebrity/celebrity-parade/2011/10/queen-latifah.html; **p56:** news.bbc.co.uk/2/hi/entertainment/304541.stm; www.spinner.com/2010/03/05/b-52s-john-lennon-yoko-ono/; **p58:** thinkexist.com/quotes/joan_baez/; jonimitchell.com/library/print.cfm?id=779; **p59:** jonimitchell.com/music/song.cfm?id=212;www.joanbaez.com/Lyrics/whereareyou.html; **p61:**www.memphisflyer.com/memphis/the-memphis-music-legacy--burden-or-blessing/Content?oid=1106497

Printed in the United States of America in Stevens Point, Wisconsin.
032013   007227WZF13

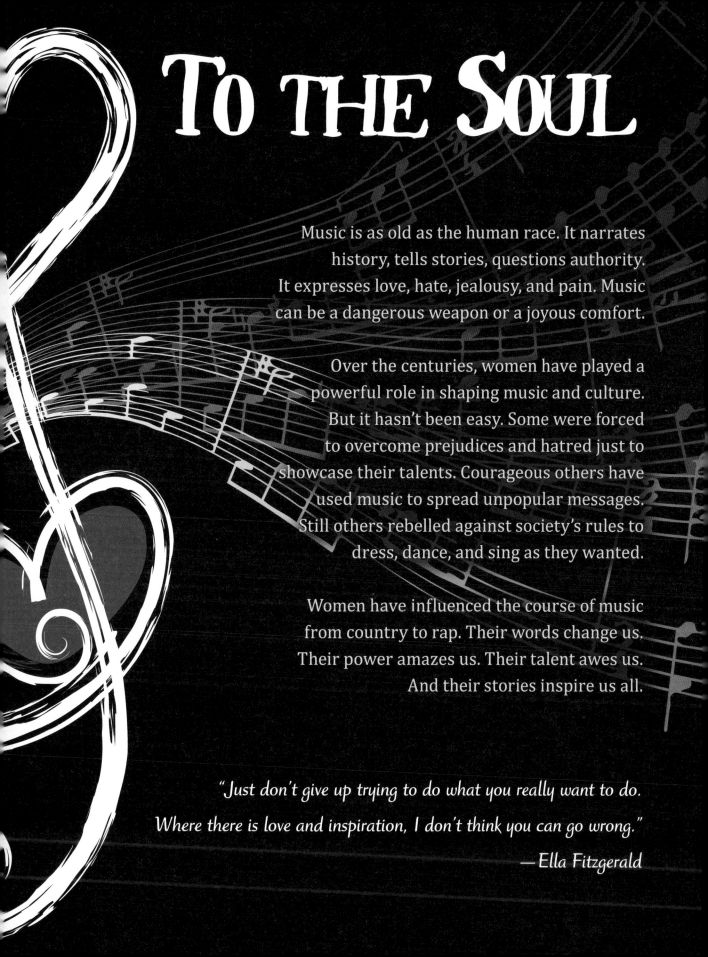

TO THE SOUL

Music is as old as the human race. It narrates history, tells stories, questions authority. It expresses love, hate, jealousy, and pain. Music can be a dangerous weapon or a joyous comfort.

Over the centuries, women have played a powerful role in shaping music and culture. But it hasn't been easy. Some were forced to overcome prejudices and hatred just to showcase their talents. Courageous others have used music to spread unpopular messages. Still others rebelled against society's rules to dress, dance, and sing as they wanted.

Women have influenced the course of music from country to rap. Their words change us. Their power amazes us. Their talent awes us. And their stories inspire us all.

"Just don't give up trying to do what you really want to do. Where there is love and inspiration, I don't think you can go wrong."
— Ella Fitzgerald

JANIS JOPLIN

January 19, 1943–October 4, 1970

I was always weird. Kids back home in Texas called me a freak and a square. So what?

Being different carved a place for me in rock and roll. No sell-out stardom for me. I was a child of the 1960s, a hippie, with a dream of being great and groundbreaking. And I was.

I was no hairspray-and-lipstick beauty. No makeup for me. My lyrics weren't about how much I wanted boys to like me. I sang about being wild, about being hurt, about taking off and seeing the world.

People said I rocked harder than most men, except maybe Jimi Hendrix. I wore ripped jeans and bandanas and smoked and drank. My voice was scratchy, rough, energetic, and vulnerable, just like me. A radio listener said I sounded like "a freight train running on loose rails."

Other women rockers noticed. They didn't have to be girly-girls and sing sweet ballads with precious soprano voices—unless that's what they wanted to do. Because of me, girl rockers knew they could be as bad as the boys. They could shriek and growl and stir up the audience with confidence and power.

On stage, away from Texas, I was the artist I wanted to be.

"Texas is OK if you want to settle down and do your own thing quietly, but it's not for outrageous people, and I was always outrageous."

Madonna

August 16, 1958–

CRITICS EXPECTED MADONNA
TO BE A 1980S ONE-HIT WONDER.
MADONNA HAD OTHER PLANS.

BIG PLANS.

Her first hits ("Everybody," "Lucky Star," and "Holiday") were sugar-coated dance tunes. An early review described Madonna's voice as "Minnie Mouse on helium." For Madonna, insults made her work harder. She took vocal lessons, developing a deeper, richer voice.

The best revenge? Success.

Madonna lives to shock and awe. Wherever she saw boundaries, she danced right through them. Outrageous behavior kept her in gossip magazines. Her reinvention of styles kept her in fashion magazines. Journalists wrote countless stories about her impact. Was she an example of independence and rebellion? Or was she teaching girls to use beauty to get ahead?

Parents shook their heads. But fans just loved her more.

Madonna's reinventions kept her career fresh. Album after album, she gave fans something new. Gospel in *Like a Prayer*. New age and electronica in *Ray of Light*. Madonna changed her image over and over. Because of her reinventions, she is one of the most recognized musicians in the world.

1989: LIKE A PRAYER

Madonna: long, dark brown hair and an attitude about religion
Music: hints of soul and gospel

1990: I'M BREATHLESS

Madonna: short curly hair and party dresses of the 1930s; performs live as 1770s royalty Marie Antoinette in a huge skirt with huge hair
Music: heavy on jazz, big bands, and some modern dance tunes like "Vogue"

1994: BEDTIME STORIES

Madonna: blonde hair with soft curls and glamorous dresses
Music: rhythm and blues

1998: RAY OF LIGHT

Madonna: long blonde hair with tight curls, exposed bras, and occasionally goth
Music: techno meets dance

2000: MUSIC

Madonna: brings cowboy hats back into style
Music: a little bit country, a little bit rock 'n roll, a lot of dance-pop

2003: AMERICAN LIFE

Madonna: shows off a yoga body and yoga skills
Music: a message album about the American dream and materialism

2009: CELEBRATION

Madonna: over-the-knee boots and top hats
Music: a greatest-hits collection of dance and pop favorites

JANET JACKSON

May 16, 1966-

Janet Jackson simply forgot the rule.

She said something about her father, and manager, in a conversation. She accidentally called him "Dad." He scolded her, "You call me Joseph. I'm Joseph to you."

This wasn't the first time Joseph had yelled at Jackson for something minor. But it was the last straw. In an emotionally charged discussion, she stiffened her backbone and fired her father. It's no mistake she released an album called *Control*.

The ambitious and stern Joseph Jackson raised Jackson and her eight siblings for the stage. Michael Jackson became King of Pop. Joseph wanted Jackson to challenge her famous brother. Jackson broke loose from her family and showed the world she was in control, that every woman should take control of her own life.

By the late 1980s, she'd become a stunning singer and trend-setting dancer. Her dancing technique drew copycat artists, and critics suggested she out-danced her brother Michael. *Rolling Stone* magazine put Jackson on its list of top 10 favorite dancers.

Her teenage voice was soft and sweet. But the grown-up Jackson began singing stronger, with more force. The album *Rhythm Nation 1814* was a runaway hit in 1989, producing seven top-five hits. She tangled her sound with rhythm and blues, funk, rap, disco, and pop. She drew fans from every corner of the music world.

TINA TURNER

November 26, 1939–

By age 45, Tina Turner had already been rich and broke, married and divorced, a superstar and a nobody.

She first soared to fame in 1960 with Ike Turner and their first album, *The Soul of Ike & Tina Turner*. When she divorced Ike in 1978, her life smashed to pieces.

The album *Private Dancer* was designed to be Turner's comeback after the tough years and poverty that followed her divorce. And it was. The album jetted Turner into the stratosphere in 1984. Fans loved her husky voice, her dance moves, her energetic shows, and the thick hair that framed her face like a lioness.

Turner showed the world there was no expiration date on girls who rock. Music journalists say Tina Turner had the biggest comeback in the history of rock and roll.

Barbra Streisand

April 24, 1942–

5 total People's Choice Awards in the categories All-Time Favorite Female Vocalist, Favorite All-Around Female Entertainer, Favorite Motion Picture Actress, and Favorite Female Musical Performer

4 key roles in the movie *Yentl*, serving as director, producer, writer, and actor

3 years of winning prime time Emmy Awards for Outstanding Individual Achievements in Entertainment—Actors and Performers, Outstanding Variety, Music or Comedy Special, and Outstanding Individual Performance in a Variety or Music Program

2 Oscars for Best Actress in a Leading Role (*Funny Girl*) and Best Original Song ("A Star is Born") AND Grammys for *The Way We Were* and *Funny Girl*

1 Cecil B. DeMille Award for outstanding contributions to entertainment

Action!

When Barbra Streisand studied herself in the mirror, she knew she'd have to rely on talent to accomplish her dreams. She wasn't going to be hired for her crooked nose and fuzzy hair.

But her voice—warm, emotional, unique, technically perfect—was her ticket to fame in the 1960s.

"I arrived in Hollywood without having my nose fixed, my teeth capped, or my name changed. That is very gratifying to me."

Streisand is the original diva. Her slow, emotional songs have ruled airwaves for decades. She was queen of ballads before Celine Dion. Her power voice could masterfully hold a note before Whitney Houston. Streisand added acting to her music career before Madonna.

Streisand pioneered technique, style, and career stretching. At the height of her fame, she was the most recognizable voice on the radio.

Most fans have never seen Streisand perform in concert. In 1967 the self-described "shy" woman forgot the lyrics at a performance. The episode haunted her.

For three decades she refused to sing for large audiences. Therapy, practice, and a teleprompter helped her return to the stage. At the end of her comeback concert, she could be heard shouting over the applause, "We did it! We did it!"

CAROLE KING

February 9, 1942–

When the curtains opened, Carole King sat gracefully at her piano. Her fingers danced across the keys. Her voice soared with emotion as she sang the words she had written. Audience members leaned close to the stage and applauded. The setting was as intimate as the music.

Long before today's rockers "unplugged" to experiment with simple, acoustic sounds, King was playing her powerful brand of message-filled melodies. In fact, rock-and-roll's history book is covered with King's fingerprints.

King spent years writing hit songs for other singers and bands.

"The Loco-Motion"
for Little Eva

"(You Make Me Feel Like)
A Natural Woman" for Aretha Franklin

"You've Got a Friend"
for James Taylor

"Will You Love Me Tomorrow?"
for The Shirelles

"Pleasant Valley Sunday"
for the Monkees

But King began to question the invisible walls in music. Why was it that singers sang, instrumentalists played, and songwriters wrote? King could do all three. And in 1971, she proved it. King wrote, sang, and recorded *Tapestry*, one of the most popular albums of all time.

King showed fans that music isn't just about snapping fingers to the beat. It's about hearing lyrics and reflecting on their meaning.

Her act—the singer-songwriter with a message—opened doors for musicians such as Sheryl Crow and Billy Joel.

Aretha Franklin

March 25, 1942–

Aretha Franklin was big, bold, and loud. She didn't ask for respect. She demanded it—in her life and in her most famous song, "Respect." Her signature song is 100 percent Aretha.

Rock and Roll Hall of Fame member and the first woman inducted

Exceptional piano player

Shaped artistically by Billie Holiday

Performed at presidential inauguration ceremonies for Bill Clinton and Barack Obama

Eighteen Grammy Awards

Called for dignity for women and anyone who has been oppressed

Trained in gospel music

By age 14, Franklin was shaking churches with her powerful gospels. But it wasn't until the 1960s when her gospel voice mixed with pop music hit the charts. Her first hit, "I Never Loved a Man (The Way I Love You)" propelled her to stardom.

Franklin's voice is purely original. She blends pop, rhythm and blues, and gospel seamlessly into her songs. Soft to assertive. Teasing to serious. Energetic to sorrowful. Aretha Franklin truly is the Queen of Soul.

Disco music and personal problems knocked Franklin off the charts, but not for long. In a smart career move, she worked on songs with younger musicians, such as George Michael and Mary J. Blige. These new songs sealed Franklin's image as a superstar and Queen of Soul.

15

FRIENDS AND LEGENDS

— Loretta Lynn
April 14, 1932–

Patsy Cline ⌐
September 8, 1932–March 5, 1963

My friend Loretta Lynn

In the 1930s, everyone was poor. Loretta and I were no different, though Loretta seemed to have it extra hard. Her dad worked two jobs so the family wouldn't go hungry. They didn't have electricity or running water. Loretta didn't even ride in a car until she was 12!

Her touching song, "Coal Miner's Daughter," told the story of her life. The honesty in her lyrics and the sincerity in her voice made her something special.

I met Loretta at the Grand Ol' Opry, the home of country music, in 1961. We took to each other right then and there. Such a talent!

Loretta didn't need me to teach her anything about writing and singing. But she was young and innocent. I feared the competition in country music might chew her up. I decided to protect her, advise her, and be her guide in this business. We became close friends.

Loretta is the country-singing train that won't quit. Country stars come and go, but Loretta's staying power and risk-taking is her legacy. A few years back, Loretta teamed up with young rock star Jack White and made *Van Lear Rose* a hit album. It introduced the Queen of Country to a whole new generation of fans.

Patsy Cline

My friend Patsy Cline

Patsy wasn't born with her famous voice, deep and rich as coffee. A childhood throat infection changed her vocal cords, and the new soulful sound made her dream of stardom.

She got married. Her husband wanted a housewife, not a wannabe star. The divorce came quick. Patsy started singing live on local radio stations. That's all it took. A record company signed her up, and pretty soon she was playing at the Grand Ol' Opry.

My voice is plainspoken and twangy. Patsy sang smooth as silk. That's the beauty of country music. You can twang, swing, and yodel, or you can sing with the voice of an angel, like Patsy. She was one of the first crossover artists. Her sound shook up honky-tonk country with little bits of blues and the new rock music. Some of her fans didn't even like country, but they sure liked what Patsy did with it.

Patsy protected and advised me. I wrote a song called "You Ain't Woman Enough to Take My Man." Those were controversial lyrics at the time, and I was worried it went too far. Patsy shook her head and told me I had a hit song on my hands. She was right.

I was heartbroken when Patsy died in that plane crash. It was 1963, and she was only 30, taken from the world too soon. We never had a chance to tour together, never recorded a song together.

I gave her a gift, though, something to take care of her memory, just like she took care of me. In 1977 I made a tribute album, *I Remember Patsy*. How could I ever forget?

Loretta Lynn

Billie Holiday

April 7, 1915 – July 17, 1959

"[Holiday's style] has been copied and imitated by so many singers of popular music that the average listener of today cannot realize how original she actually was."

—bandleader Artie Shaw

During the Great Depression, everybody was desperate for work—including me. Some friends told me that bars were hiring dancers to bring in customers. I could dance a little, so I auditioned at a Harlem bar. The manager said I was terrible. I needed work so bad I told them to forget the dancing. I sang them two songs, and they hired me for $2 a night.

After that I had decent crowds at the jazz clubs. But it was the musicians—Teddy Wilson, Lester Young, Benny Goodman—who really noticed me. They connected me to business people, and soon I was makin' records.

I mixed up the sounds of big band, blues, and jazz. People wondered how my voice could be mellow but packed with such emotion. Smooth then gritty. Rhythmic then off beat. I told them,

"I hate straight singing. I have to change a tune to my own way of doing it. That's all I know."

All the performers gave each other nicknames. They called me "Lady Day," the greatest jazz singer ever.

Compliments made me soar. When I was a kid, compliments were rare. In fact, my whole life was hard. No education, no money. But there was plenty of violence and racism for black people. But my singing seemed to push through that color barrier. I was one of the first black women to sing with a white orchestra.

I loved to sing powerful ballads, and people must have liked them too. My records made money, and concerts sold out. I really worked to convey the meaning of every song because really that's what jazz is all about.

Fast Facts

- Holiday had no musical training and never learned to read music.
- "What a Little Moonlight Can Do" and "Miss Brown to You" were her first hits.
- Her real name was Eleanora Fagan.
- Holiday used music to convey powerful messages. Her most famous songs include "Strange Fruit," "God Bless the Child," and "Gloomy Sunday."

Whitney Houston

August 9, 1963–February 11, 2012

She didn't mean to overshadow the Super Bowl. All she was supposed to do was sing the national anthem. But what happened was bigger than anyone dreamed.

The New York Giants and the Buffalo Bills were poised for an epic Super Bowl battle. The stadium in Tampa Bay that day in January 1991 bulged with fans. Millions more were glued to their TV screens. Whitney Houston stood before a backdrop of flags, military flyovers booming overhead.

Houston was already a star. Her 1985 debut album sold 25 million copies worldwide. With her second album she became the only artist ever to have seven consecutive #1 hits, surpassing a record previously set by the Beatles and the Bee Gees. So it was no surprise she had been invited to sing at the Super Bowl.

Super Bowl XXV was played just 10 days after the United States entered the Persian Gulf War. People were tense, worried about their nation and the service people fighting far from home. So when Houston's voice flooded the packed stadium, the country heard hope.

With her gospel-inspired style and soaring notes, Houston sang the national anthem as no one ever had before. One reporter said her performance "was as close to perfect as a human voice can get." A recording of her version of the song became the fastest-selling single in her record label's history. That day, Houston elevated herself from pop star to musical icon.

Timeline

Clive Davis hears Houston perform at a nightclub. He signs her to the Arista label on the spot.

Releases her first album, which sets the record as the highest selling debut album by a solo artist.

Releases her second album, making history as the first female artist to enter the *Billboard* album charts at #1.

1983

1985

1987

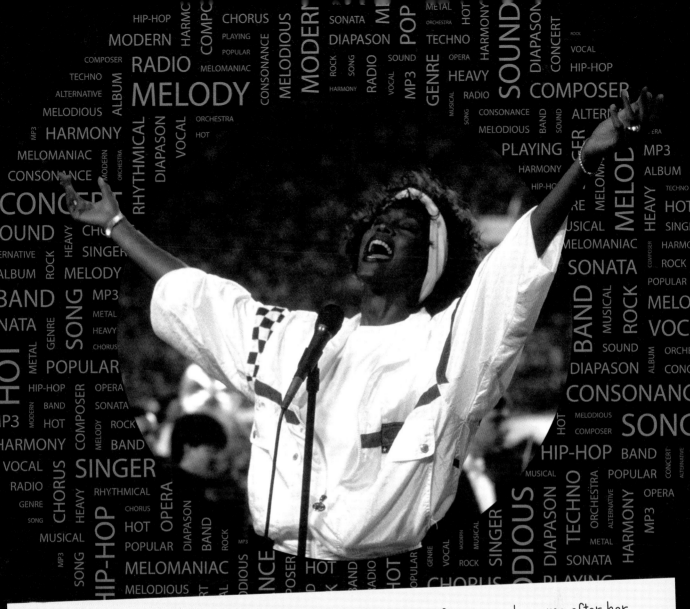

Whitney Houston was often called the Prom Queen of Soul. She had a near perfect voice that astounded audiences. Her effortless, powerful vocals made her one of the world's best-selling artists. Houston's voice and style influenced a generation of singers who came after her. Christina Aguilera and Celine Dion have followed in her diva path. Mariah Carey sounds so much like Houston that when she debuted, many thought she was Houston.

Stars in the hit movie *The Bodyguard*. The movie's sound track features six of Houston's songs and becomes the highest selling motion picture sound track album in history.

Houston dies holding *The Guinness Book Of World Records* title as music's "most awarded female artist of all time." She earned 411 awards, including two Emmys, six Grammys, 16 *Billboard Music Awards*, and 23 American Music Awards.

1992

2012

Opera Queens

Maria Callas
December. 2, 1923–September 16, 1977

Young Maria Callas had a flair for opera. She was so skilled that her mother moved the family from New York back to their native Greece. The move gave Callas a rare opportunity to study in opera's classical tradition.

Callas soared in the European opera scene. Opera is dramatic by nature, but Callas raised the bar. She sang with such emotion and expression that she overshadowed her peers.

Callas' star status enabled her to take on a personal cause. She wanted to save rarely performed operas. Operas such as *Lucia di Lammermoor*, *La Traviata*, and *Anna Bolena* challenged the world's greatest singers. Operas that hadn't been staged in more than 60 years returned because of Callas' persistence.

Beverly Sills

May 25, 1929 – July 2, 2007

Even non-opera fans adored Beverly Sills. Her popularity prompted Johnny Carson, king of late-night TV, to invite her to be the show's guest host. An opera singer at the helm of *The Tonight Show*? That's not all. Sills even appeared on the *Muppet Show*.

Sills jumped from fine art to pop culture and back again. Her down-to-earth nature seemed to conflict with the elegant, high-society world of opera. But her voice did not.

She had a warm soprano voice. Still, she sang with power, and her voice slid beautifully between notes that were difficult to blend.

THE GO-GO'S

CHARLOTTE CAFFEY
(VOCALS, KEYBOARDS)
OCTOBER 21, 1953–

KATHY VALENTINE
(BASS)
JANUARY 7, 1959–

BELINDA CARLISLE
(VOCALS)
AUG. 17, 1958–

JANE WIEDLIN
(GUITAR, VOCALS)
MAY 20, 1958–

GINA SCHOCK
(DRUMS)
AUG. 31, 1957–

In the 1970s and 1980s, punk music filled bars. Rockers with rainbow-colored hair, mohawks, piercings, and tattoos pounded out hard-edged, angry songs. The beats were harsh but simple, and the lyrics were full of protest.

Belinda Carlisle loved the punk scene. One day, she chatted outside a bar with a friend. They shared a dream of starting their own band in the male-dominated punk world.

"We had both the guts and the enthusiasm, plus some additional craziness, and as we sat on the curb, we talked one another into a froth of excitement," Carlisle said.

"Everybody we knew was in a band. Why not us?"

But their band didn't just jump on the bandwagon. The Go-Go's shook up the punk scene. They injected punk with the sound of California surf music. In a flash, The Go-Go's brand of punk "lite" was on every radio across the country.

Their energy, gutsy attitude, and catchy beats inspired a generation of all-girl groups, such as the Bangles and Bananarama. The Go-Go's proved female musicians didn't need a man writing their songs or wailing on guitar.

The Go-Go's rocketed to fame with lightning speed. The band became a California club favorite before they'd even mastered their act.

- At their first show, they didn't know how to plug in their speakers and instruments.

- Jane Wiedlin learned guitar during rehearsals and shows. She put masking tape on the guitar frets to help remember the chords.

- Charlotte Caffey wrote the hit song "We Got the Beat" in less than five minutes.

- When singer Belinda Carlisle listened to one of their first live recordings, she was horrified by her terrible vocals.

The oldest Anderson girl had a gift. I can still remember the sound. Her voice rose high as our church steeple then dipped so low the whole congregation shivered. Marian. Her name was Marian.

Her mom was too poor to pay for music school, so one day the other church ladies and me had an idea. We passed the church basket a second time so that girl could buy lessons from a real professional.

Best donation we ever made.

Marian's first performance was at the New York Philharmonic in 1925. Then it was Carnegie Hall and across Europe. She sang with orchestras. Spirituals and jazz and parts of famous operas. President Franklin Roosevelt and his wife Eleanor invited her to sing at the White House.

Our girl had hit the big time.

But it wasn't easy. Marian couldn't stay in whites-only hotels. She had to sit in the colored section on trains.

In 1939 Marian was going to sing at Constitution Hall, owned by the group Daughters of the American Revolution. They said absolutely not, no black singers allowed. Eleanor Roosevelt was so disgusted she resigned from that group. The first lady set up a different concert for Marian at the Lincoln Memorial.

Marian was a worldwide star. If she couldn't pick her own hotel, then think how bad it was for regular black people. I guess you could say the world's biggest star put the biggest spotlight on racial injustice.

Yup, best donation we ever made.

Marian Anderson

February 27, 1897–April 8, 1993

PROMINENT PLAYERS

BONNIE RAITT

November 8, 1949–

Bluesy guitar player since the 1960s

"… electric guitar, for me, has the raunch and the beauty that more openly reflects the range of emotions I want to get when I'm singing and playing. It's much more expressive to me. And that's what keeps me going back."

"Even though she's been inducted into the Rock and Roll Hall of Fame, Bonnie Raitt is still vastly underrated both as a singer and a guitarist. That's because, without making any fuss about it, she hasn't been willing to conform to anyone's expectations."

—*Rolling Stone* contributing editor Anthony DeCurtis

TORI AMOS

August 22, 1963–

Unique and classically inspired pianist since the mid 1980s

"It plays me, really, I don't play it. There is surrender to what the instrument is capable of, and I try and listen to it; really listen to it. Every piano—the notes, the sound of the relationships—is unique."

"She helped turn the piano into a rock instrument, showed that she can create big hits in different genres, and challenged every critic who ever tried to put her in a box."

—Neil Tevault on NPR, August 2011

JOAN JETT

September 22, 1958–

Defiant and forceful guitar player since 1975

"My guitar is not a thing. It is an extension of myself. It is who I am."

"A no-nonsense player who in only a few strums can get an entire barroom howling her 1982 hit, 'I Love Rock 'n' Roll.'"

— Julie Vadnal, *ELLE* magazine, 2009

28

NANCY WILSON

March 16, 1954–

Energetic and sophisticated guitar player since 1974

"[The song] 'Angie' became my calling card. I'd go down to the local music store, Bandwagon, and play that song on the better guitars, and people would be impressed. It was my first feeling of what it would be like to have an audience."

"Nancy Wilson holds a special place in the annals of rock guitar: as a player, singer, and songwriter for Heart, she brought her acoustic vision to the rock 'n' roll table and demanded to be heard."

—Julie Bergman, *Acoustic Guitar*, September 1999

MEG WHITE

December 10, 1974–

Simple and primal drummer since 1997

"People have a lot to say about Meg White's drumming, and though there are fancier drummers out there, the way she played built the White Stripes' foundations, and the energy between them, the force, the bond, something that was a little deeper, a little darker than love, made them utterly compelling."

—Laura Barton, *The Guardian*, February 3, 2011

NORAH JONES

March 30, 1979–

Mellow and jazz-infused pianist since 2002

"Without a piano I don't know how to stand, don't know what to do with my hands."

"She played electric and acoustic guitar at several junctures in the set, including for 'Come Away With Me' and 'Lonestar,' but 'Don't Know Why' again proved Jones really belongs at the grand [piano]."

—Pierre Perrone, *The Independent*, January 15, 2007

Ella Fitzgerald

April 25, 1917– June 15, 1996

WHEN ELLA FITZGERALD SANG, SHE

SQUEALED LIKE A TRUMPET,

moaned like a bass,

and wailed like a saxophone.

Fitzgerald joked, *"I stole everything I ever heard, but mostly I stole from the horns."*

In the 1940s, big bands turned into small bands, and the singer's voice led the group. Nobody memorized notes. Ella and her musicians made it up and mixed it up. Her voice came to define a new jazz sound—bebop jazz.

Jazz scholar Vincente Minnelli said, *"If you want to learn how to sing, listen to Ella Fitzgerald."* That's exactly what artists did. Etta James, Aretha Franklin, and Natalie Cole all credit Fitzgerald as their inspiration and the perfect study for improvisation.

Fitzgerald's journey to singing sensation was as bumpy as gravel. Her father abandoned the family, and her mother died young. Problems plagued her teenage years. Eventually she ended up in a tough juvenile hall. After running away, Fitzgerald lived on the streets. Desperate to be a performer, she entered a singing competition at a Harlem theater in 1934. Fitzgerald won first prize and a ticket to stardom. Bandleader Chick Webb saw Fitzgerald's performance and knew he'd discovered a star.

She zoomed to fame: 200 records, 13 Grammys, a National Medal of Arts, and the Kennedy Center Honors Award. Fitzgerald was even honored with her own U.S. postage stamp—an American symbol for an American icon.

My Fair Julie

STARRING
JULIE ANDREWS

October 1, 1935-

Broadway singer Julie Andrews' voice was a rare gem. Trained singers often cover two octaves. Andrews' voice could cover an amazing four octaves. She starred in some of Broadway's biggest shows. Audiences loved her soaring voice and sincere performances. And the cast admired her team spirit. Julie rejected a Tony Award nomination in 1996 for *Victor/Victoria*. She believed the selection committee overlooked the outstanding work of the show's cast and crew.

Andrews stretched her career from theater to film. She won lead roles and awards in her film career, but she loved the energy of Broadway musicals. Her singing career, however, ended on a surgeon's table. In 1997 Andrews had surgery to repair damage done by years of singing. The medical team injured the part of her vocal chords responsible for her unforgettable voice.

Theater Highlights

1954	*The Boyfriend*
1956	*My Fair Lady*
1960	*Camelot*
1993	*Putting It Together*
1995	*Victor/Victoria*

Call Me Ethel!

STARRING
ETHEL MERMAN

January 16, 1908–February 15, 1984

Ethel Merman worked as a secretary to support herself until Broadway opened its doors for her. In 1930 she landed the lead in *Girl Crazy*. Her success in the show launched her Broadway career. With her booming, animated voice, she quickly became a huge star who spent decades dazzling theatergoers. Merman performed her role in *Panama Hattie* 501 times.

Theater Highlights

1930–1931	*Girl Crazy*
1939	*Stars in Your Eyes*
1940–1942	*Panama Hattie*
1950–1952	*Call Me Madam*
1956–1957	*Happy Hunting*
1959–1961	*Gypsy*
1964–1970	*Hello, Dolly!*
1966	*Annie Get Your Gun*

The Time of Patti LuPone's Life

STARRING
PATTI LUPONE

April 21, 1949–

Powerhouse singer Patti LuPone almost didn't make it through one of Broadway's most challenging vocal roles. Starring as Eva Perón in *Evita*, the difficult score caused LuPone to lose her voice. To protect her singing voice, she remained silent whenever she wasn't onstage—for 19 months. Her commitment and talent made LuPone not just one of Broadway's biggest stars, but its hardest-working star.

Theater Highlights

1974	*Next Time I'll Sing to You*
1975	*The Robber Bridegroom*
1979–1983	*Evita*
1997–1998	*The Old Neighborhood*
2005–2006	*Sweeney Todd*
2008	*Gypsy*
2010–2011	*Women on the Verge of a Nervous Breakdown*

Patti LaBelle

May 24, 1944–

Her voice plunged into deep, mellow sounds. A second later it hit notes few opera sopranos could reach. Her voice was nasal then pure, low then soaring. But always powerful.

Patti LaBelle's volcanic voice has influenced dozens of singers. Artists with great vocal range, such as Whitney Houston, Christina Aguilera, and Mariah Carey, adopted LaBelle's fluttery singing style.

In LaBelle's early career, she led the band LaBelle. They were the first African-American band to be on the cover of *Rolling Stone*. But the band's popularity waned as glam rock, with its flashy clothes and makeup, took center stage. The band had to change if it was going to survive.

The band tossed out its old-school image and focused on hot fashion and suggestive lyrics. And it worked. "Lady Marmalade," about a hot-as-lava woman from New Orleans, was a huge hit. The message: artists have to keep up with trends or learn how to redefine them.

In the late 1970s, the group began to crumble. So LaBelle struck out on her own. Her singles climbed the charts. The ballad "The Best is Yet to Come" earned LaBelle her first Grammy nomination as a solo act. Later, she would win two Grammys.

"Lady Marmalade," one of LaBelle's most energetic songs, has been covered by four separate artists: Christina Aguilera, Lil' Kim, Mya, and Pink. Some critics would say that none measure up to LaBelle's energy and golden voice.

SELENA

April 16, 1971–March 31, 1995

EVEN NOW, AFTER ALL THESE YEARS, PEOPLE WANT TO KNOW WHAT HAPPENED MARCH 31, 1995, IN ROOM 158 OF THAT MOTEL.

I know, of course. And so does Yolanda Saldivar. The motel staff saw me fall, bleeding from a gunshot wound. They heard me whisper, "Yolanda." They saw the ring clutched in my hand. The friendship ring from Yolanda.

The newspapers told part of my story.

April 1, 1995, Corpus Christi, Texas—Tejano superstar Selena-Quintanilla Pérez, simply known as Selena, was shot and killed yesterday. Police arrested Yolanda Saldivar, a friend who ran the star's fan club, for Selena's murder.

Police reports say the 23-year-old singer contronted Saldivar at a Corpus Christi motel about money missing from the fan club and boutiques. The stores were owned by Selena and managed by Saldivar.

The women argued, and Saldivar shot and killed Selena according to eyewitness accounts.

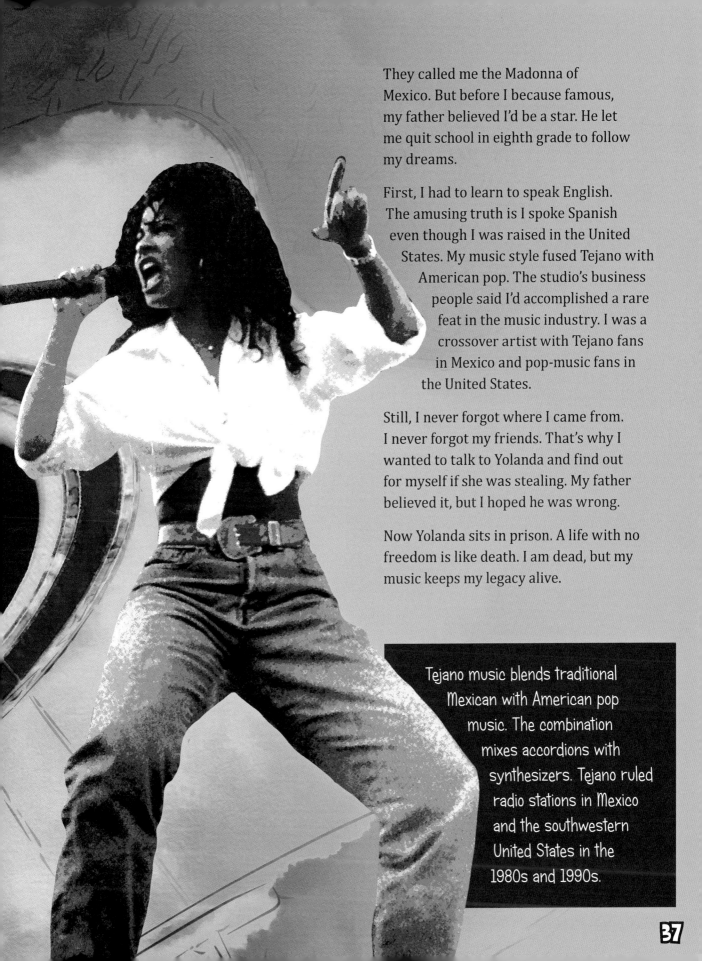

They called me the Madonna of Mexico. But before I because famous, my father believed I'd be a star. He let me quit school in eighth grade to follow my dreams.

First, I had to learn to speak English. The amusing truth is I spoke Spanish even though I was raised in the United States. My music style fused Tejano with American pop. The studio's business people said I'd accomplished a rare feat in the music industry. I was a crossover artist with Tejano fans in Mexico and pop-music fans in the United States.

Still, I never forgot where I came from. I never forgot my friends. That's why I wanted to talk to Yolanda and find out for myself if she was stealing. My father believed it, but I hoped he was wrong.

Now Yolanda sits in prison. A life with no freedom is like death. I am dead, but my music keeps my legacy alive.

Tejano music blends traditional Mexican with American pop music. The combination mixes accordions with synthesizers. Tejano ruled radio stations in Mexico and the southwestern United States in the 1980s and 1990s.

Rock 'n Roll FASHIONISTAS

Rock 'n roll isn't just guitars and drums. It's attitude. It's a rebellion against the norm. Rock trendsetters love to shock.

HOT-PINK BIKINI SHIRTS

PURPLE HAIR

THE MINIEST OF MINI SKIRTS

ALLIGATOR BOOTS

These female musicians impressed with music and dress. Their albums blazed new trends in music, and their creative closets launched new looks.

Cyndi Lauper

June 22, 1953–

Cyndi Lauper was a feisty 1980s singer who turned her body into a colorful canvas. Orange and pink hair. Neon eyeshadow. Polka dots mixed with stripes. Three belts and 14 necklaces—all in one outfit. For Lauper, the clothes reflected her colorful, zany personality. Teenage girls quickly adopted Lauper's love of extras. Dressing wasn't just clothes. The look was unfinished without bright makeup, belts, scarves, and retro jewelry.

"I loved the whole [retro glamour look], but I always liked the idea of making it my own, so I wore high heels and pedal pushers, which nobody was really wearing at the time. Then I would wear a vintage '40s top that didn't quite go with my hair or anything for that matter. I would try anything."

LADY GAGA

March 28, 1986–

Lady Gaga went from nobody to superstar in 2008. Not just another sun-soaked blond, she turns heads and makes statements with her wardrobe. She collected music awards wearing a red lace dress that covered her entire face. Another time she wore a dress made of beef.

"There's this one pair of shoes I've had for years, and they cost like $25. I have such an emotional attachment to the shoes that every time I see them, I can hear the fans and feel the bass coming through the bottom of the stage."

GRACE JONES

May 19, 1948–

Grace Jones had a string of dance-club hits, fusing disco with a hint of reggae. Her fashion sense was sometimes boyish and usually bizarre—metallic hats, black lipstick, a cat's mask, even a dress made of cardboard.

"My look is for girls on the run. I'm always in a hurry. For me, sunglasses are eye make-up, even at night. Half of my face is sunglasses, the other half is lips—I use four colors to do my lips, My other trademark I suppose is the hood."

Gladys Knight

May 28, 1944–

They call Gladys Knight the "Empress of Soul." I guess that makes me, Merald "Bubba" Knight, the brother of the empress. I've been her backup singer and business partner for 50 years.

Gladys never had the lungs like Whitney Houston or Patti LaBelle, but she had charisma and an expressive voice. You could hear Gladys on the radio, just playing as background music, and you'd know what she'd be singing about. Love, hate, joy, loss, desire ... it all came through because she was either an actress who sang or a singer who acted. We had a new sound—Gladys' low voice, very earthy and mature, in a world of sopranos.

When we were kids, Gladys and I had two lives. We sang in the church choir in the morning. At night we performed in smoky clubs. The club managers would have us sit in the car until it was time to play because we were so young. We'd sneak up the back steps and then sneak back out to sit in the car until the second show.

It was the 1950s, and our parents got flack for letting kids live a church-to-club life. But we landed a record deal when I was 15 and Gladys was 13. Gladys was the front woman, and my cousins and I were the Pips. We toured with Jackie Wilson and Sam Cooke before Gladys could drive a car.

We hit the top, slid to the bottom, then soared again. That's life in the music business, and nobody's weathered the roller coaster like us. As Gladys likes to say, "We've shared hot dogs, and we've shared caviar."

My sister and I still make music together.
The hot dogs and caviar don't matter much.
It's the music that matters.

DEBBIE HARRY

July 1, 1945–

Musically speaking, Debbie Harry has a split personality.
She's the lead singer for the band Blondie.
And she's Debbie Harry, a solo gig.

BLONDIE

Both acts have had a 30-year career.

	BLONDIE	DEBBIE HARRY
MUSIC SOUND	PUNK MEETS NEW WAVE MEETS RADIO-WORTHY POP	SIMILAR TO BLONDIE, BUT FUNKIER AND MORE EXPERIMENTAL
CONFLICT OR CONTROVERSY	DEBBIE GETS ALL THE ATTENTION.	LESS SUCCESS AS A SOLO ARTIST
INFLUENCED	BANGLES, THE GO-GO'S, CONCRETE BLONDE	MADONNA, LADY GAGA, PINK
MOMENTS OF NOTE	THEIR SONG "RAPTURE" WAS THE FIRST MEGA-HIT IN THE UNITED STATES WITH RAP LYRICS.	RANKED #12 ON VH1'S 100 GREATEST WOMEN OF ROCK 'N ROLL

Debbie Harry was the face of Blondie. Fans and critics marveled over her bombshell image and talent. But frustration bubbled over for the other members of the band. Harry was so popular, many people thought she was Blondie. Band members grew tired of feeling invisible. At one point, they wore buttons that said, "Blondie is a band."

GIRL GROUPS THAT ROCK

Before there were girl bands, there were girl groups. And the difference is huge.

Girl groups dominated 1960s radio. They performed sweet, innocent songs in beautiful harmonies. With matching dresses and perfectly styled hair, they sang and swayed to choreographed moves.

THE SHIRELLES

(left to right) Addie "Micki" Harris, Shirley Owens, Doris Coley, and Beverly Lee

The Shirelles get credit for launching girl-group popularity. Their hit "Tonight's the Night" opened the gates. The Shirelles had 11 top-40 songs. Beatles legend John Lennon counted them among his favorite bands. The group sang sweet, innocent songs about love in flawless harmony. The Shirelles' success convinced business executives young girls would spend huge amounts of money on girl-group records. In a six-year period, beginning in about 1960, an estimated 800 girl groups released songs.

DIANA ROSS AND THE SUPREMES

(top) Diana Ross
(left to right) Florence Ballard, Mary Wilson, and Betty McGlown

Diana Ross and the Supremes ruled Motown Records in the mid-1960s. The legendary recording company mixed soul with popular music, creating a new style. With lovely gowns and perfect hairdos, the Supremes projected sophistication and style. Ross' wispy voice led the group, whose sound was neither entirely black nor entirely white. Unlike most girl groups, the Supremes had a long shelf life. They made Motown mainstream, no longer a company for mostly black audiences.

THE RUNAWAYS

(left to right) Lita Ford, Joan Jett, Jackie Fox, Sandy West, Cherie Currie

The Runaways built the bridge between girl groups and girl bands. The five young women played their own instruments and ditched the innocent girl-group image. They were bad girls and proud of it. Their sound was a chaotic mix of hard rock, metal, and punk. It was an explosion of electric guitar and drums.

The Runaways pushed boundaries. Teenage girls in jeans and T-shirts were singing about a party lifestyle. Mainstream Americans didn't like it, but the band's rebellious attitude became the inspiration for a new wave of girl bands.

Girl groups opened doors for girl bands. Girl bands spawned rockers who played instruments, wrote songs, produced their own work, and sang about independence, strength, and challenging authority.

ANNIE LENNOX

December 25, 1954–

Lennox snipped her hair to the scalp and dyed it red. She wore leather and men's suits.

BOLD

SASSY

BRILLIANT

Annie Lennox and Dave Stewart were the Eurythmics. Inspired by punk, their new wave style was radio-friendly because of its smoother, electronic sound. Lennox sang, wrote songs, and played keyboards. She created a bold image that paired perfectly with her husky, powerful voice.

Other new wave bands faded, but the Eurythmics shook up their sound, stretching from hypnotic electric beats to the richness of soul.

As a solo artist, Lennox's soulful vocals and stylings were a change from the electronic sound of the Eurythmics. But her haunting, powerful songs proved she was a serious artist.

Lennox has a bold, powerful stage presence. But she wasn't always that confident. In fact, for years she was overcome by shyness. At her first flute lesson, Lennox was so shy, she vomited on the teacher's floor.

But if she wanted to be a star, she knew she had to conquer her fear. Lennox used a mind trick. When onstage, she pretended she was in costume, playing the role of another singer. As she got older, she was able to stop playing the game and overcome her shyness.

Is the group a legend because they were the first all-girl rap group?

Is it because they infused pop music into their act and attracted a mainstream audience?

Or is it their long shelf life in an industry filled with one-hit wonders?

Salt-N-Pepa

The 1980s launched hordes of male rappers. Female rap artists were just dots on the rap map. But audiences craved rap from a female perspective, and soon that map started to change.

Together, Salt-N-Pepa, Queen Latifah, MC Lyte, and Monie Love burned through the doors of the rap industry. Tired of the portrayal of women in rap, they turned lyrics upside down.

Salt-N-Pepa preached independence, respectful relationships, self-esteem, and girl power. Beautiful and flirty, their looks attracted men while their messages moved women.

The group still tours and draws crowds. Twenty-plus years later, Salt-N-Pepa is still breaking new ground.

Sandra "Pepa" Denton
November 9, 1969~

Deidra "DJ Spinderella" Roper
August 3, 1971~

Cheryl "Salt" James
March 28, 1966~

49

SINGING OUT

SHERYL CROW

Sheryl Crow adopted environmental awareness as a personal cause. And she's not shy about it. She shares her views with fans, reporters, and, occasionally, government leaders.

When Crow visited Washington, D.C., she saw a key advisor to President George W. Bush. Angry about the administration's environmental policy, she confronted the official about global warming and other issues. The man didn't want to talk. He said, "I don't work for you. I work for the American people." Crow retorted, "I am the American people!"

February 11, 1962–

SARAH MCLACHLAN

It was 1997, and women had nabbed all of the top five spots on *Billboard's* end-of-the year list of best sellers. Yet female rockers struggled to find spots on tours and festivals. Promoters—mostly men—didn't believe women drew big audiences. McLachlan decided to prove them wrong. She founded Lilith Fair in 1997, a festival tour with only women rockers. And she did prove them wrong: That year, Lilith Fair was the country's best-selling concert.

McLachlan is also a well-known animal-rights activist. She has been the face of the American Society for the Prevention of Cruelty to Animals (ASPCA) for several years.

January 28, 1968–

When stars champion a cause, fans take note. Art can prompt people to think about issues in different ways.

Some of music's biggest acts have fought for change, sometimes risking their popularity and careers.

PINK

Personal beliefs mean more to Pink than titles, even royal titles. An animal-rights activist, Pink confronted the heir to Great Britain's throne in a letter. Prince William was rumored to be spending his 21st birthday in Africa, learning to track animals and hunt with spears.

She'd already posed in an anti-fur ad for PETA, spoke against animal testing, and lectured circus lovers about the abuse of elephants. She had no problem scolding a future king.

September 8, 1979-

ANI DIFRANCO

Ani DiFranco sells the usual merchandise at her shows—CDs, T-shirts, and such. But at election time, there's an extra table. DiFranco urges fans to register to vote before they leave the show. "I still very much believe the trouble with the American democracy is we haven't tried it yet," DiFranco said. "We have the lowest voter turnout of any industrialized nation." In 2004 she even coordinated a get-out-the-vote tour in swing states.

September 23, 1970-

51

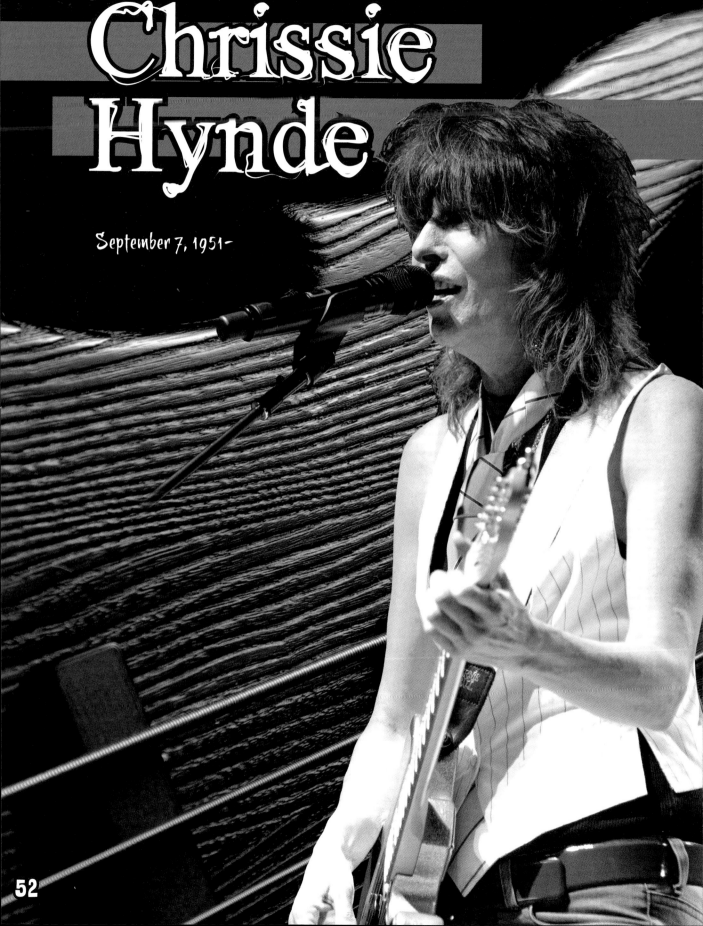

Chrissie Hynde

September 7, 1951-

Don't talk to Chrissie Hynde about influencing a generation of female rockers. She rebels against being a rebel.

"I'M NOT A FIGUREHEAD FOR ANYTHING. I WAS A SINGLE MOM WITH TWO KIDS. WHAT ELSE WAS I GOING TO DO? IT WAS EITHER BE IN A BAND OR BE A WAITRESS."

It was 1979. Bubblegum pop was taking over radio, but Hynde didn't like pretty. She's blunt, uncompromising, and she had no problem telling industry executives to get out of her face.

Hynde was one of the first women to take complete control of the stage: husky-voiced singer, songwriter, and guitarist. Her act was Chrissie Hynde and The Pretenders. But she was, without question, the bandleader.

Other women rockers took note of Hynde's old-school rock act. Even though they had different styles, artists like Courtney Love, Madonna, and Salt-N-Pepa adopted Hynde's attitude. Those women broke the rules and crossed the lines of acceptable behavior. They swore, took political stands, and ignored reviews.

For decades, many male rockers pushed rock's boundaries and played bad attitudes like an instrument. For Hynde, it was no act. She is the real deal.

Tracy Chapman

March 30, 1964 —

In the 1980s, young listeners rejected the protest music of Joan Baez and Joni Mitchell. Synthesizers, catchy beats, and fun lyrics defined the new sound.

Then a quiet folk musician strummed her way from coffee houses to mainstream radio. With dreadlocks and a deep, rumbling voice, Tracy Chapman burst into the white world of folk music. Chapman isn't the first African-American folk singer. But she is the most successful.

Raised by a single, working-class mother, Chapman expressed herself with music. When she was just 8 years old, her mother gave her a guitar. Chapman immediately began writing songs. Soon her songs began to reflect what she was learning. Her teachers at school were politically active, and Chapman absorbed ideas about injustice and activism. Her lyrics focused on poverty, racism, and violence.

Chapman's message music opened the eyes of a generation growing up with songs like "Everybody Have Fun Tonight (Everybody Wang Chung Tonight)." Some African-American artists and fans criticized her appeal to white audiences. They claimed she was out of touch with her own community.

But others disagreed. Nelson George, a black music critic for *Billboard*, said, "Tracy Chapman is the most important artist of this year [1988] and may end up being one of the most important artists of the next 10 years."

George was right, with one exception. Chapman's influence—so far—has spanned more than 20 years.

Queen Latifah

March 18, 1970–

Eight-year-old Dana Owens flipped through the pages of a name book. Latifah. It jumped from the page. Latifah, meaning delicate, sensitive, kind, and nice. That's how Dana saw herself.

From that moment on, friends and family called her Latifah. When she started ruling the world of rap, she became Queen. A commanding name for a commanding woman.

Queen loved the rap beat, but she saw herself as a rap poet. She was interested not just in rhymes, but in raps with meaning and emotion. And that wasn't the only thing that made Queen different.

In 1980 rapping was for men. The thought of the day was that women didn't rap. They just danced in rap videos.

For the Queen, that wasn't good enough. Queen persisted as a performer and showed industry executives that people were hungry for a new twist on rap. She preached that women should stick together and show their independence. As she climbed the charts, other female rappers had a path to follow.

"People paved the way for me and [I paved] the way for others. You have to expand the game as much as you can for the ladies. I've always kind of been a champion for the ladies in that sense."

Queen also stomped on rap's definition of beauty—thin and curvy women wearing skimpy clothes. She's a role model for larger women, urging them to be proud of their bodies.

Queen Latifah's brand is about self-respect. With the empire she's built, her stage name deserves to be Queen.

YOKO ONO

February 18, 1933–

Critics and fans say Yoko Ono may be the world's strangest artist.
EVER.

She was an artist before meeting her famous husband, singer-songwriter John Lennon. They recorded together in the 1960s, and Ono was introduced to the world.

The world was puzzled.

Yoko screeched, moaned, and chanted wordless vocalizations.

"She's shaped nothing, she's contributed nothing, she's simply been a reflection of the times."

—Brian Sewell, art critic for the *London Evening Standard*

Ono shrugs off the criticism. People just don't get her. Yoko embraced experimenting with art forms in new ways. Even non-fans admitted she was bold and interesting.

Many bands admired her unique style because she didn't write or play cookie-cutter music. Bands who wanted to be different, even a little weird, took note, such as the Talking Heads and the B-52's.

"Yoko was such an inspiration for us in the early days."

—B-52's guitarist Keith Strickland

Love her or hate her, Yoko Ono is an unforgettable figure in the history of rock and roll.

Grace Slick was equal parts **ATTITUDE** and **TALENT**. She introduced music fans to acid rock, which had long solos, distorted electronics, and less focus on lyrics. Both as a solo act and member of Jefferson Airplane, Slick injected politics into music. She had strong opinions, and she shared them on and off stage.

Her songwriting was cutting edge and shocking, and so was her behavior.

She played onstage without a shirt.

She drag raced on the Golden Gate Bridge.

She tried to confront President Richard Nixon, but security stopped her.

For Slick, politics had a home in music. She fused them together and showed the world that musicians could—and should—call attention to injustice, poverty, and other world problems.

GRACE SLICK

October 30, 1939–

MUSICAL POETS

Consider the 1960s a cultural volcano. War raged in Vietnam, and young Americans demanded it end. African-Americans took to the streets and demanded civil rights. Women wanted equality too. College campuses became centers of philosophy and debate. America's youth wanted to change the world.

And a resurrection of folk music led the way. Modern folk has a simple sound without the bells and whistles of mainstream pop. Sometimes called "message music," folk music called for change with lyrics and guitars.

JOAN BAEZ
January 9, 1941-

Joan Baez meant to be shocking. Her lyrics were a call to action. Audiences found Baez's voice beautiful but haunting, a style that called attention to her messages.

Baez sang about the day's issues, but she also got involved. Bold, opinionated, and fearless, Baez marched with civil rights demonstrators and sang at their protests. One year, she refused to pay taxes in opposition to military spending. After that, she joined migrant farmworkers in the fields to support fair wages.

Police arrested her at protests, and she would serve her short sentences. Then she'd jump back into the movement and tell the world what she thought.

"I've never had a humble opinion. If you've got an opinion, why be humble about it?"

JONI MITCHELL
November 7, 1943-

A rich, expressive voice combined with song writing, guitar playing, and strong political beliefs made Joni Mitchell the perfect 1960s folk package. More comfortable with small audiences than the media, Mitchell had a knack for creating conversations at her shows.

Mitchell is widely considered a key figure in the 1960s counterculture. But she didn't see herself that way. She felt her songs were more poetry than protest.

"I've written only one protest song. That was 'Urge for Going,' which was a protest song against winter. And it certainly isn't going to stop winter."

Mitchell didn't mean to be shocking. Some might say her lyrics fit the times. But Mitchell suggested that the times simply fit her lyrics.

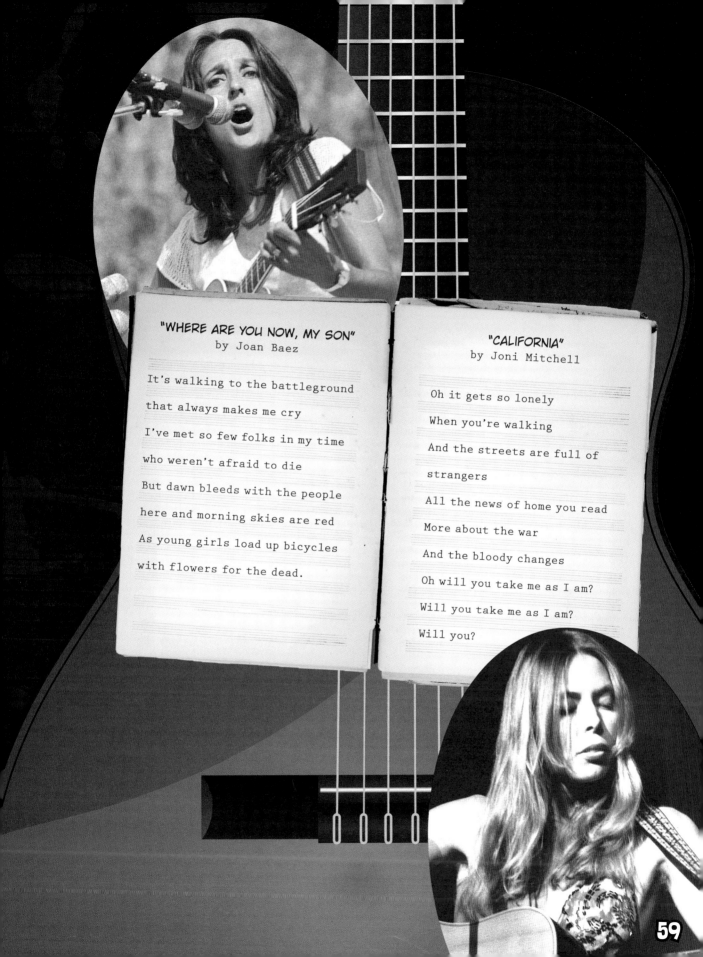

"WHERE ARE YOU NOW, MY SON"
by Joan Baez

It's walking to the battleground

that always makes me cry

I've met so few folks in my time

who weren't afraid to die

But dawn bleeds with the people

here and morning skies are red

As young girls load up bicycles

with flowers for the dead.

"CALIFORNIA"
by Joni Mitchell

Oh it gets so lonely

When you're walking

And the streets are full of

strangers

All the news of home you read

More about the war

And the bloody changes

Oh will you take me as I am?

Will you take me as I am?

Will you?

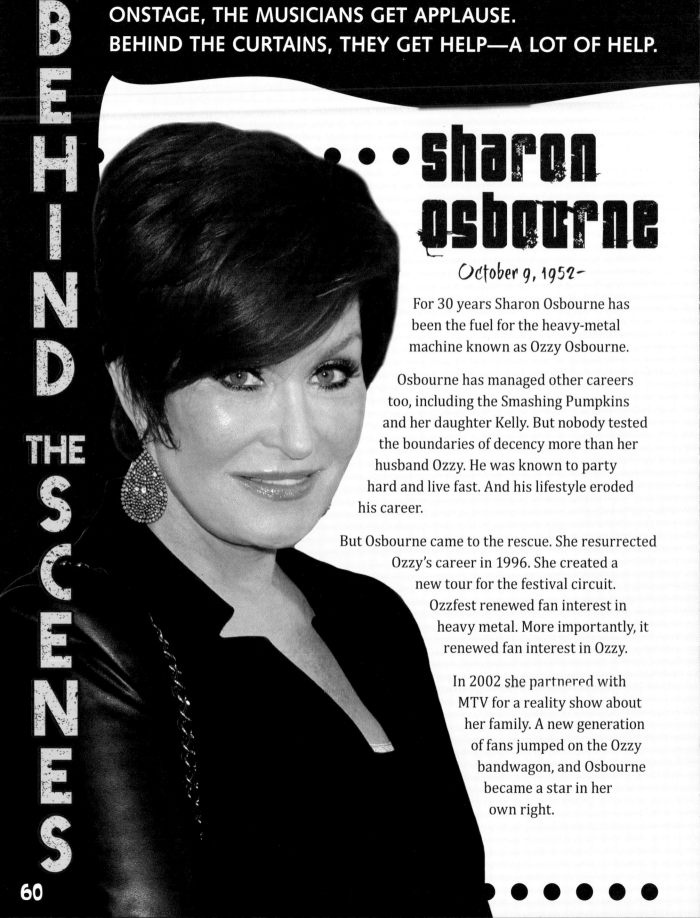

ONSTAGE, THE MUSICIANS GET APPLAUSE.
BEHIND THE CURTAINS, THEY GET HELP—A LOT OF HELP.

···sharon osbourne

October 9, 1952–

For 30 years Sharon Osbourne has been the fuel for the heavy-metal machine known as Ozzy Osbourne.

Osbourne has managed other careers too, including the Smashing Pumpkins and her daughter Kelly. But nobody tested the boundaries of decency more than her husband Ozzy. He was known to party hard and live fast. And his lifestyle eroded his career.

But Osbourne came to the rescue. She resurrected Ozzy's career in 1996. She created a new tour for the festival circuit. Ozzfest renewed fan interest in heavy metal. More importantly, it renewed fan interest in Ozzy.

In 2002 she partnered with MTV for a reality show about her family. A new generation of fans jumped on the Ozzy bandwagon, and Osbourne became a star in her own right.

cordell jackson

July 15, 1923–October 14, 2004

Cordell Jackson founded Moon Records in 1956. Women were singing in those days, but they weren't seen or heard in the engineering booths. Until Jackson came along.

Sun Studios—the company that made Elvis a star—rejected Jackson's request to record. But that didn't keep her from shining.

She started her own company, Moon Records. She famously declared that she "aimed for the sun but landed on the moon."

Jackson opened doors for women to be producers and engineers. She showed them engineering was just another piece in the puzzle of rock and roll. And women could work on any piece they wanted.

Jackson was also an accomplished singer and electric guitar player. Many called her the "Rockin' Granny."

Barrier Breakers

The women in this book represent the dreams, successes, and struggles of music's most fascinating artists. Trailblazing musicians shared the challenge of smashing barriers. From jazz to punk to rap, the walls crumbled. Today's young female artists stand on the shoulders of the women who destroyed those barriers.

The stories of all the talented female musicians in the world can't be told in one book. But their message can be summed up in two words:

Girls Rock!

1930s
ETHEL MERMAN MARIAN ANDERSON

BILLIE HOLIDAY ELLA FITZGERALD

1940s
MARIA CALLAS

1960s
ARETHA FRANKLIN

TINA TURNER LORETTA LYNN

THE SUPREMES JANIS JOPLIN

BEVERLY SILLS GRACE SLICK

GLADYS KNIGHT JOAN BAEZ

YOKO ONO JONI MITCHELL

BARBRA STREISAND

1950s
CORDELL JACKSON

PATTI LABELLE JULIE ANDREWS

PATSY CLINE THE SHIRELLES

1970s
THE RUNAWAYS

CAROLE KING BONNIE RAITT

PATTI LUPONE GRACE JONES

NANCY WILSON CHRISSIE HYNDE

DEBBIE HARRY

1980s
CYNDI LAUPER

WHITNEY HOUSTON JANET JACKSON

THE GO-GO'S JOAN JETT

SALT-N-PEPA ANNIE LENNOX

TRACY CHAPMAN SHARON OSBOURNE

SELENA MADONNA

QUEEN LATIFAH

2000s
LADY GAGA

NORAH JONES PINK

1990s
ANI DIFRANCO MEG WHITE

TORI AMOS SHERYL CROW

SARAH MCLACHLAN

INDEX

READ MORE

Guillain, Charlotte. *Music: From the Voice to Electronica.* Timeline History. Chicago: Heinemann Library, 2011.

Schwartz, Heather E. *Girls Rebel!: Amazing Tales of Women Who Broke the Mold.* Girls Rock! North Mankato, Minn.: Capstone Press, 2014.

Ziegler, Robert. *Great Musicians.* DK Eyewitness Books. New York: DK, 2008.

INTERNET SITES

FactHound offers a safe, fun way to find Internet sites related to this book. All of the sites on FactHound have been researched by our staff.

Here's all you do:

Visit *www.facthound.com*

Type in this code:
9781476502342